.

paperblanks®
JAPANESE LACQUER
BOXES

Notre couverture illustre une boîte laquée japonaise du XIXème siècle, réalisée durant la période Edo ou Meiji. Cet artisanat consiste à peindre de la sève sur des objets pour les protéger et les améliorer. La boîte originale, laquée selon le style Maki-e, utilise de la poudre métallique pour créer de fastes conceptions et atteste du talent humain à créer de la beauté de sources improbables.

Unser Bucheinband zeigt die Malerei auf einem japanischen Lackkasten aus der Edo-Zeit oder Meiji-Periode zeigen. Die Lackkunst entsteht dadurch, dass Gegenstände mit Baumsaft bemalt werden, um sie zu schützen und zu verschönern. Die Original-Box, hergestellt im Maki-e Style, wurde mit Metallpuder bestreut, damit die Designs prächtiger wirkten.

Questa copertina ritrae una scatola giapponese del periodo Edo o Meiji. La laccatura è l'arte di proteggere e valorizzare gli oggetti preziosi tingendoli con un estratto vegetale. La scatola originale in stile Maki-e, i cui disegni sono stati realizzati con polvere metallica, conferma la capacità umana di creare bellezza con pochi mezzi.

Esta cubierta reproduce una antigua caja lacada japonesa del periodo Edo o Meiji. El lacado es el arte de pintar savia sobre objetos preciados para protegerlos y decorarlos. La caja original de estilo Maki-e utiliza polvo metálico para dar vida a lujosos diseños, y refleja la habilidad humana para crear belleza a partir de materiales insólitos.

paperblanks®
JAPANESE LACQUER
BOXES

Karakusa

Our journal cover features the image of an antique 19th-century Japanese lacquer box from the Edo or Meiji period. Lacquerware is created by painting tree sap onto treasured objects to protect and enhance them. The original box, lacquered in the Maki-e style, uses metallic dust to create luxurious patterns and is evidence of the uniquely human ability to create beauty from unlikely sources.

ISBN: 978-1-4397-5039-1
MINI FORMAT   176 PAGES   UNLINED
DESIGNED IN CANADA

Photograph by Kenji Yamazaki.
Printed on acid-free sustainable forest paper.
North America 1-800-277-5887
Europe 800-3333-8005
Japan 0120-177-153

paperblanks.com